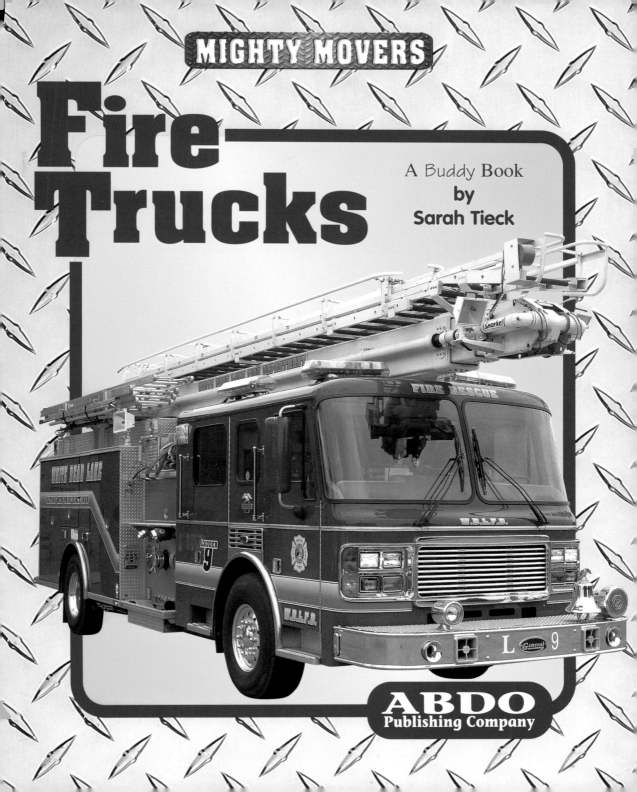

VISIT US AT
www.abdopub.com

Published by ABDO Publishing Company, 4940 Viking Drive, Edina, Minnesota 55435.

Printed in the United States.

Written and Edited by: Sarah Tieck
Contributing Editor: Michael P. Goecke
Graphic Design: Maria Hosley
Image Research: Sarah Tieck
Photographs: Terry Hellige, Photos.com
Special thanks to the White Bear Lake Fire Department.

Library of Congress Cataloging-in-Publication Data

Tieck, Sarah, 1976-
   Fire trucks / Sarah Tieck.
      p. cm. — (Mighty movers)
   Includes index.
   ISBN 1-59197-828-9
      1. Fire Engines—Juvenile literature. I. Title.

TH9372.T54 2004
628.9'259—dc22

                                        2004050238

Table of Contents

What Is A Fire Truck?

A fire truck is an emergency vehicle. Firefighters drive fire trucks. Firefighters ride to a fire in a fire truck. Fire trucks are called fire engines, too.

A fire truck carries tools to help put out fires. It has a loud siren that makes noise on the way to a fire. Most fire trucks are red. Some fire trucks are yellow. The color yellow helps people see the truck at night.

A fire truck leaves the fire station.

PARTS OF A FIRE TRUCK

Ladders

Fire fighting equipment

Gauges and valves

Inside the cab.

In the driver's seat.

Warning lights

Fire hose

Siren

What Do Firefighters Do?

Firefighters work in a fire station. When the alarm sounds, they get dressed and slide down the fire pole. Then, they get into fire trucks and rush to the fire. Firefighters are trained to put out fires. Firefighters also help to save people's lives.

Firefighters extinguish fires using tools on the fire truck.

Firefighters work together to put out a fire.

What Do Fire Trucks Do?

Fire trucks carry the supplies firefighters need to do their jobs. Fire trucks carry hoses and tools such as an ax or a sledgehammer. These tools help to extinguish fires. Tools and hoses help firefighters do their jobs.

There are many different kinds of fire trucks. Some trucks carry water. Some trucks carry tools. Some trucks carry hoses. Each truck does a different job.

Fire trucks carry special equipment to fight fires.

Hook-and-Ladder Trucks

Hook-and-ladder trucks are used to put out fires in tall buildings. Firefighters climb the truck's long ladder. The ladder helps the firefighters rescue people trapped in a burning building. It also lets them get closer to fight the fire.

This truck lifts firefighters closer to the fire.

Some hook-and-ladder trucks are so long they need two drivers. These are called tiller rigs. Tiller rigs have two parts. This is so the long truck can turn sharp corners.

One driver steers the front of the truck. A second driver sits in a cab at the back end of the truck. The second driver has a steering wheel, too. This steering wheel turns the wheels in the back. The drivers talk to each other on a radio about driving the truck.

Firefighters use ladders to rescue people.

Water Trucks

Tanker trucks carry water to extinguish fires. Pumper trucks carry water, too. But, pumper trucks have a part called a pump. The pump uses air pressure and engine power to make water spray farther.

Firefighters use hoses to spray the water on the fire. Hose wagons carry hoses.

There are also trucks called foam units. Foam units put out fires that cannot be extinguished by water. These fires are called chemical fires. Foam units spray a special chemical that extinguishes the fire.

Pumper trucks spray water.

17

History Of Fire Trucks

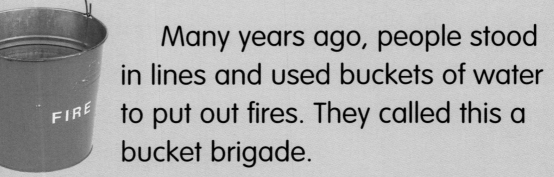

Many years ago, people stood in lines and used buckets of water to put out fires. They called this a bucket brigade.

The first fire trucks were simple carts. People would pull the cart to a fire. Then, they would pump water to fight the fire.

In the 1800s, firefighters used horses to pull steam engines to a fire. The steam engines helped pump more water onto fires.

This is an antique fire truck. It is no longer used to fight fires. It has old-fashioned tools and equipment.

Steering wheel

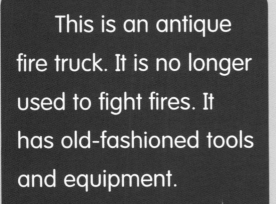

Antique ladder and firefighting tools

Fire Trucks Today

The fire truck's bright lights flash as it races to the fire. The sirens make a loud noise. The lights and sirens help warn other drivers. The fire truck moves fast to get to the fire.

People first used fire trucks with motors in the 1900s. Now, all fire trucks have a motor. Fire trucks help save lives. They also make it easier to put out fires.

Firefighters drive to fires with lights flashing.

A fire hydrant.

Fire hydrants help firefighters fight fires. Fire hydrants are located on streets. Firefighters hook the hose into the fire hydrant. Fire hydrants supply water to help fight fires.

Important Words

chemical fire a type of fire that can't be put out with water.

emergency vehicle a truck or car that is used to help with events such as fires, sicknesses, or accidents.

extinguish to put out.

foam unit special fire extinguisher that puts out a chemical fire.

rescue to save from danger.

supplies things that are needed to do something.

Web Sites

To learn more about fire trucks, visit ABDO Publishing Company on the World Wide Web. Web site links about fire trucks are featured on our Book Links page. These links are routinely monitored and updated to provide the most current information available.

www.abdopub.com

Index